Robots Today,
Robots Tomorrow

Written by Hannah Reed

Flying Start
to Literacy®

T0363506

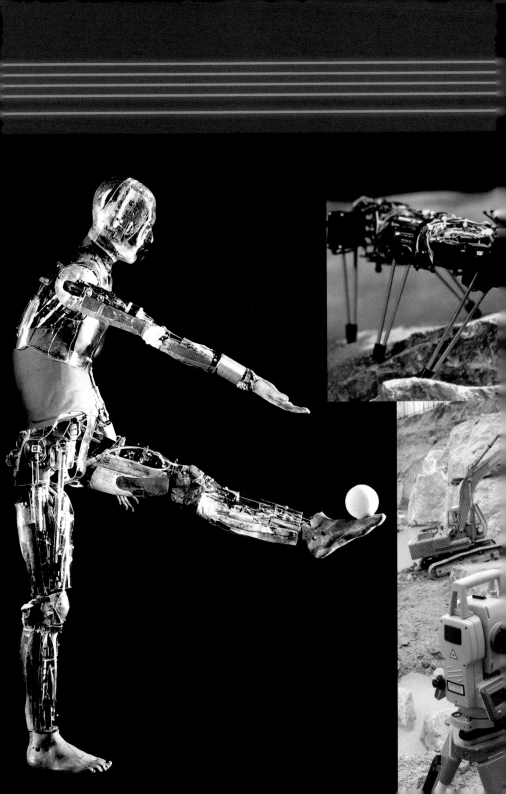

Contents

Introduction

New robots are being invented all the time.

Robots are machines that do jobs that are difficult or dangerous for people to do. Many of these robots help people to do their jobs more easily.

Some robots help people who are sick or injured.

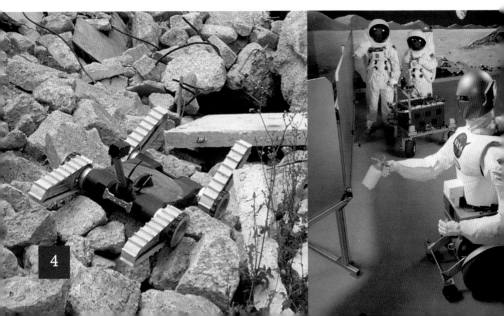

Robot farmers

Many farmers have to spray poison on the slugs that eat their crops. This costs a lot of money and the poison gets into the food.

A robot called SlugBot has been invented. It can catch slugs on crops and get rid of them.

SlugBot has a camera that can see slugs. It can tell the difference between slugs and other things it sees.

SlugBot can pick up slugs with its robotic arm and put them in a tank. Inside the tank, the slugs are turned into fuel. The fuel keeps SlugBot going.

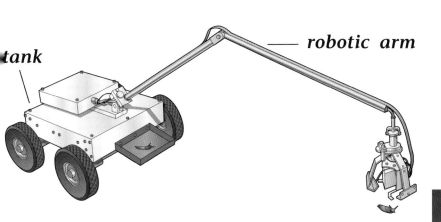

tank

—— *robotic arm*

Robot horses

People use horses to carry things over rocky or uneven ground. They walk with the horses to show them the way. This is not always safe or easy for the people or the horses.

A robot that can walk over uneven ground has been invented. It is called BigDog. BigDog has four legs and can carry heavy loads.

The robot is still being tested, but in the future this kind of robot might be used to carry heavy loads in places where there are no roads at all.

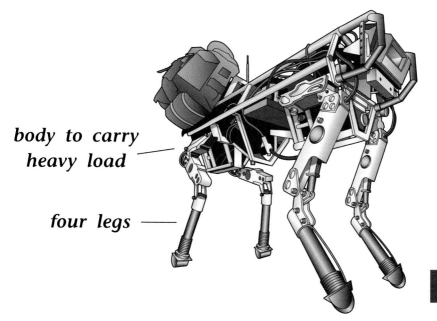

body to carry heavy load ——

four legs ——

Robots to the rescue

Sometimes, a tremor under the ground can make the ground shake. This can make houses fall down and trap people under rubble. Rescuers try to find trapped people by using long poles that have cameras and microphones on them.

These poles cannot go around corners, so finding people is very difficult.

A robot has been invented that can go around corners and crawl into narrow spaces. This robot is called Snakebot.

In the future, it will be used to help rescuers find trapped people more quickly.

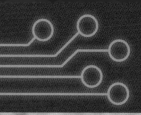

Working in the deep sea is difficult for people. A robot has been invented that can take photos and measurements in the deep sea. It can move on its own under water where people cannot go easily.

flotation tanks to keep robot upright

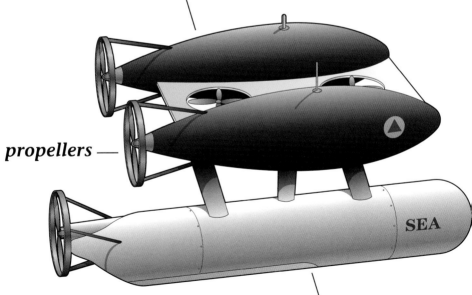

propellers —

SEA

14

This part collects information

The robot sends information to computers. These computers are on nearby ships. Scientists collect the information and find out about the deep sea without having to go underwater themselves.

People are trying to make this robot better so that it can send information around the world.

Robots in medicine

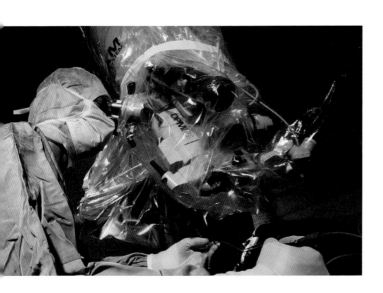

Sometimes, robots are used to operate on people. Doctors control the robot and decide where the robot will cut and what it will do.

Small cameras on the robot show the doctor exactly what is happening during the operation.

A medical robot only needs to make
a small cut to go inside a person's body.
This means that there is less bleeding,
and the patient can get better
much faster.

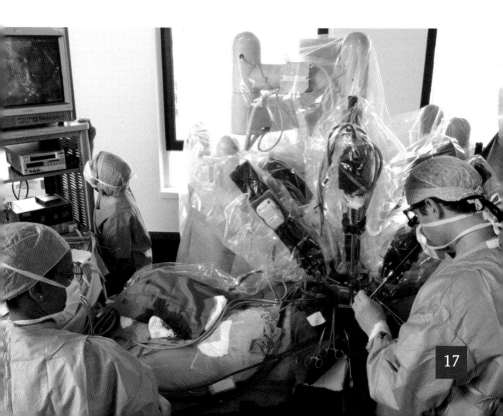

Robots that are used in operations can also be controlled by computers from far away.

This means that a doctor can be in one hospital and operate on a patient in another hospital by controlling a robot.

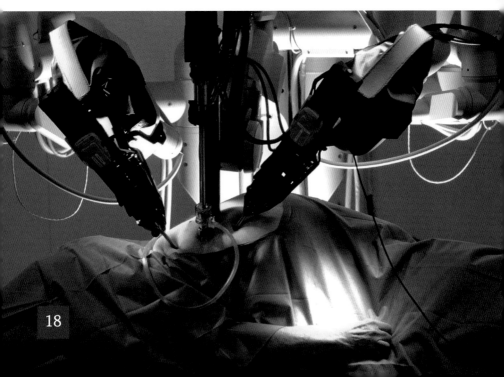

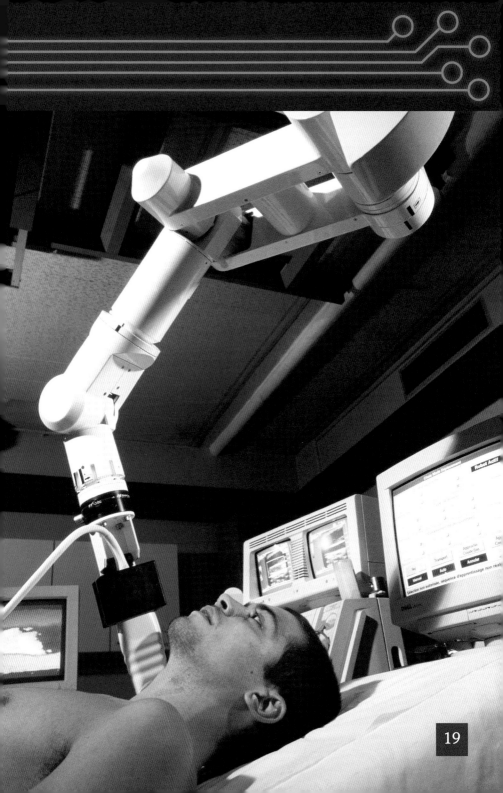

Robotic arms

Sometimes, people need robotic arms. A robotic arm can do simple tasks such as picking up something.

Robotic arms can be controlled by makin small chest and neck movements.

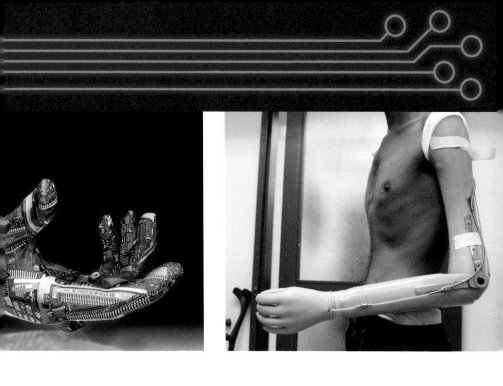

Scientists are testing a new robotic arm that can be controlled by a person's brain.

When the person with the robotic arm thinks about what they want the arm to do, the arm will do it.

This robotic arm might be able to do all the things that a real arm can do.

Conclusion

Robots can do amazing things.

In the future, robots will be used to do more and more work that is dangerous or difficult for people to do.

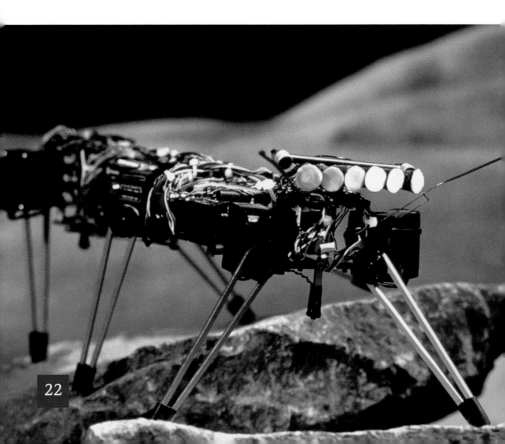

23

Index